POWERFUL PEOPLE ARE POWERFUL IT PROFESSIONALS

A  Book

POWERFUL PEOPLE ARE POWERFUL IT PROFESSIONALS

YOUR DAILY GUIDE TO BECOMING A POWERFUL INFORMATION SYSTEMS PERSON

A "Power Series" Book

Peter Biadasz, Richard Possett
and
Wayne L. Anderson

A  Book

iUniverse, Inc.
New York Lincoln Shanghai

POWERFUL PEOPLE ARE POWERFUL IT PROFESSIONALS
YOUR DAILY GUIDE TO BECOMING A POWERFUL INFORMATION
SYSTEMS PERSON

iUniverse books may be ordered through booksellers or by contacting:

iUniverse
2021 Pine Lake Road, Suite 100
Lincoln, NE 68512
www.iuniverse.com
1-800-Authors (1-800-288-4677)

The views expressed in this work are solely those of the author and do not necessarily reflect the views of the publisher, and the publisher hereby disclaims any responsibility for them.

ISBN-13: 978-0-595-41753-7 (pbk)
ISBN-13: 978-0-595-86093-7 (ebk)
ISBN-10: 0-595-41753-1 (pbk)
ISBN-10: 0-595-86093-1 (ebk)

Printed in the United States of America

"Anything the human mind can conceive
and believe it can achieve."

Napoleon Hill

Dedications

I dedicate this book to those who know computers are a great tool, but are constantly frustrated by this amazing technology.

—Peter Biadasz

To the wonders of the mind constructively produced and utilized to advance humankind to the ultimate.

—Richard Possett

I dedicate this book to the many system professionals whose job is difficult on a good day. These professionals are required to work in a world that is changing at an exceptionally rapid rate. Their devotion to the profession has provided technologies that have altered the direction of businesses and entire industries. They transformed many companies from *shops* to major corporate players in the fiercely competitive business landscape.

—Wayne L. Anderson

Acknowledgements

Thank you to my family, my friends, and business associates; you add so much to my personal and professional life. Even though I may not always show it, know that my appreciation runs very deep. (Yes, I have said this before but one can never say it enough.)

—*Peter Biadasz*

I would like to propose a special wassail to my partner, Wayne Anderson, for his considerable share in the making of this book. I truly appreciate his hard and smart work. Thank you!

—*Richard Possett*

I want to thank my wife, Pam, who played the role of subject matter expert, editor, consultant and sometimes conscience. She provided a great deal of encouragement and support during the creation of the manuscript. In addition, a book like this could never come to fruition without the help of a large number of people. Many IT professionals with whom I have worked over the years have provided me with the experiences and inspiration that were the basis for this book.

—*Wayne L. Anderson*

Why Read This Book?

POWERFUL PEOPLE ARE POWERFUL IT PROFESSIONALS: *Your Daily Guide to Becoming a Powerful Information Systems Person* is the book that will add power to your information technology (IT) career. It is easy for you to find books about the technical aspects of IT; however, a book that describes how to improve the systems professional (i.e. *you*) has been hard to find … until now.

Do you want to know more about how to become a powerful person? Of course you do. The *real* power, however, is not in having physical strength. To be a truly powerful system professional, you need the ability to get the job done more efficiently; improve your working relationship with your business partners; and improve you as a professional. You need to have the capacity to motivate teams, create relationships, and influence people. You must have a vision and the ability to communicate that vision. In addition, you need the skill to empower others to be their best. A really powerful IT professional models powerful behaviors and inspires others to take action. That is the expertise that this book will provide you.

This book is unique because it is multidimensional. It is *practical*, *inspirational* and *educational* all at the same time. It is a workbook that is designed to strengthen your career as a system professional. Although the book is comprehensively powerful, it is still simple and easy. It provides you with daily quotations from some of the most successful people in the world which makes it simple to read. It also presents you with a wide-range of assignments that are easy to complete. When you research the authors, you will become a well-rounded individual. As a result, you will have the skills necessary to be a strong IT professional.

As you progress through this book, you will discover both your good and bad habits. You developed these habits over a long period of time. They were developed in both your personal and professional life. By reading this book and completing the assignments you will grow more powerful each day by building on your strengths; eliminating your weaknesses; and developing *new* habits that are the behaviors of successful and powerful people.

This book also has a bonus feature. It provides you with the ability to add depth to your skills. You will actually go through the material twice. You will complete the lessons in the first six months and add to your work in the following six months. This process will give you a chance to critique your development and make the appropriate adjustments. Read the quote; complete the assignment; apply one skill each day; and you will have no choice but to develop into a powerful systems person. You will reap the wonderful rewards both in, and outside, of your workplace. You will become the *powerful* information technology person that we already know you can be!

Table of Contents

Preface

Information technology is becoming so pervasive that it is having a significant impact on a company's strategy and operations and therefore, stock price and investor relations. In some cases, the continued existence of a company is solely dependent on its ability to successfully implement information technology solutions. Today, with increased global competition, extremely rapid advances in technology and the subsequent growth in customer knowledge and sophistication (partly as a result of that technology), companies must change and change quickly. It takes focused, organized and well prepared IT professionals to help companies to respond to this environment. This book was created to equip the IT professional with mental tools they need to meet this challenge.

The principles in this book have been born of long and productive business and information technology careers. We walk the talk. We practice what we preach. We are confident that the quotations in this book will inspire you to do the same. It should take you beyond mediocrity on the job and at home. As they are completed, the daily lessons will make you a more dynamic information system professional. Please complete each daily lesson in order to significantly improve your personal and professional life. We pray that you have a great day and a better tomorrow as you grow your way to being an awesome person and more effective IT professional.

Peter Biadasz, Richard Possett and Wayne L. Anderson

(Before proceeding, turn to pages 191-192 to read more about the authors and gain a better frame of reference and perspective regarding this book.)

Introduction

What Is An IT Professional?

IT professional are people who are called upon to perform exceptional tasks on a daily basis. He or she is required to simultaneously understand technology; understand the industry; understand the company and implement solutions that satisfy an enterprise's strategic direction. They are often asked to deliver these solutions in a timeframe that is shorter than what it took to create the original strategy. In most cases, the solutions that they develop must be correct the first time. Their solutions may be keeping a plane in the air, maintaining a production line of a major corporation in operation, switching the tracks on which commuter trains are running, transferring billions of dollars across international bank accounts, influencing the decisions of major government officials or monitoring the status of a nuclear reactor.

As an IT professional, you are a powerful person. You are powerful because each day you use your knowledge and expertise to change the way we live. Your talents allow us to move faster, work smarter, maintain contact with each other and perform our routine tasks more easily. You are a steadfast innovator that takes complex concepts and ideas and transforms them into powerful tools used by most people. The more powerful you are as an IT professional, the more influential you will be in your career and personal endeavors. The more influential a person you become, the more powerful an IT professional you will be.

What (Or Who) Is A Powerful Person?

A powerful person is anyone who has influence over another person. Notice that we said influence, not control. Many people misunderstand power as a control issue. Whether you know it or not, you influence many people every day. It may be as obvious as your interaction with a co-worker or a family member or as subtle as your mannerisms when standing in a long checkout line at the store. In every circumstance, especially in the workplace, where another person can observe you, you are exerting influence by word and/or by example. This book will address the characteristics that you show to the people in your life. These are the same characteristics that these same people look at when determining how powerful a person you are to them. The powerful people quoted in this book were powerful because of their influence on others, even you. You may have never met any one of these individuals, just as you may not have met many of the people that you have affected, either positively or negatively.

In the margin of this page take a minute now and list the most powerful influences in your life, especially the IT Professionals who have influenced you the most. This is where your powerful lifestyle example begins.

How to Use This Book

Everyday you are given the opportunity to be more proficient in a skill that leads you to become a more powerful IT professional. Read the daily quote and then thoughtfully complete the task presented. You will need more room to write many of the assignments and will perhaps want to reflect on many others. Therefore, a daily journal will be very helpful or just use additional paper. By doing so, you will become a more powerful IT professional.

Six Months Review

The six months review gives you the opportunity to add depth to what you have learned and to the task that you had started—and hopefully—completed earlier. This is critical to ensure that personal and system professional habits, not just actions, are created and reinforced. At the end, you will find that you have addressed all of the major areas that make you a more powerful IT professional.

To reinforce certain key points, you may see a topic covered more than once. Note that this is a key topic requiring your thorough and honest attention.

Sample Illustration

January 1
July 2

"There is no such thing as saturation in education."

Thomas Watson

Note the names of two System Professionals that you know who seem to continue to be current with technology and highly value education. Contact them for a meeting to discuss learning and staying up on technology. During the meeting ask them how they managed to balance work, family and education.

Name: *Albert Smither*

Action: *Telephone Al to schedule a luncheon meeting to discuss his views on staying up on technology through learning.*

Name: *Maria Youngman*

Action: *Contact Maria at the next staff meeting and set-up a meeting with her to explore technology learning and education in general.*

Six Months Review:
I had lunch with Al and he feels that learning is a lifelong quest for new ideas. Remaining open to new ideas has kept him pursing technology education as well as personal development. I met with Mary and she believes that one cannot advance without keeping up with technology through a dedicated learning plan. Her passion for knowledge has caused her to seek ways of balancing family, work, and educational pursuits.

About The Quote Sources

If you want to receive more rewards from these daily exercises, perform research on the people quoted in these pages. You are encouraged to learn about their life and times. Learning how these individuals became powerful people in their own right will be a great reward. If a person is quoted more than once, research the circumstances in which each quote has occurred. In the instances of sayings and proverbs a study into the traditions associated with each source may be of benefit. The results of your research can be placed in the lines provided labeled as "Quotation Source Information."

And please remember:
"The wisdom of the wise, and the experience of the ages,
may be preserved by quotation."
Benjamin Disraeli

Tell me … I'll forget.

Show me … I'll remember.

Involve me … I'll comprehend.

Be great but get better!

BE A POWERFUL IT PROFESSIONAL!

Important Note

Please understand that in instances in which a quote refers to "him," "his" or "man" does not imply a specific gender. Substitute the correct gender where appropriate.

Daily Quotes for Powerful Leadership Success

January 1
July 2

"All the rivers run into the sea; yet the sea is not full."

Solomon

One of the primary ways in which a systems professional can become successful is to develop strong business relationships. Like many rivers flowing into the sea, you can never have too many relationships. The more you develop, the more you have. Your sea will never get full.

List some ways that you will acquire and develop business relationships:

_____
_____
_____
_____
_____

Name and contact the people who you think are good at developing strong business relationships. Determine which techniques you will adopt:

_____
_____
_____
_____
_____

Six Months Review:

_____
_____
_____

Quotation Source Information:

_____
_____
_____

January 2
July 3

> "If you don't know where you are going,
> you will probably wind up someplace else."

Yogi Berra

Many systems professionals spend more time preparing for a family vacation than they do their careers. They move through their career[s] without really knowing where they are going. The odds of being successful in any endeavor significantly increases when a person has written goals. Ninety eight percent of successful people have written goals. You should plan to join that elite group.

Write down your top three professional goals:

_____

_____

_____

List the most successful IT professionals that you know and learn how they became successful:

_____

_____

_____

_____

_____

Six Months Review:

_____

_____

_____

Quotation Source Information:

_____

_____

_____

January 3
July 4

"The secret of success is constancy of purpose."

Benjamin Disraeli

Develop some steps that you will take to stay focused on your professional objectives:

1. _____
   _____

2. _____
   _____

3. _____
   _____

Contact two people who you admire for their ability to stay focused on their objectives and learn what they do:

1. _____
   _____

2. _____
   _____

Six Months Review:

_____
_____
_____

Quotation Source Information:

_____

_____

_____

January 4
July 5

"For those to whom much is given, much is required."

John F. Kennedy

List the top five things that others have provided you in order to ensure your success:

1. _____
   _____

2. _____
   _____

3. _____
   _____

4. _____
   _____

5. _____
   _____

Six Months Review:

_____
_____
_____

Quotation Source Information:

_____
_____
_____

January 5
July 6

"The only way to make a man trustworthy is to
trust him."

Henry Lewis Stimson

Develop some steps that you plan to take to increase the trust that your
coworkers will have in you:

1. _____
   _____

2. _____
   _____

3. _____
   _____

Contact two people who you think are the most trusting people you
know. Learn their system for trusting other professionals.

1. _____
   _____

2. _____
   _____

Six Months Review:

_____
_____
_____

Quotation Source Information:

_____

_____

_____

January 6
July 7

"Drama is life with the dull bits cut out."

Alfred Hitchcock

We often expect our professional lives to be like what we see on television and in the movies. This causes us to be surprised when real life happens. What are the three things that you can do to ensure that you are viewing your professional life realistically?

1. _____
   _____

2. _____
   _____

3. _____
   _____

How will you validate your approach?
_____
_____
_____

Six Months Review:
_____
_____
_____

Quotation Source Information:
_____
_____
_____

January 7
July 8

> "After all, when you come right down to it,
> how many people speak the same language
> even when they speak the same language?"

Russell Hoban

Name steps you will take to make certain that you are communicating well with the business and technology people who you come in contact with today.

1. _____

2. _____

3. _____

4. _____

5. _____

How will you confirm that your process is effective?
_____
_____
_____

Six Months Review:
_____
_____
_____

Quotation Source Information:

_____

_____

_____

January 8
July 9

"There is nothing quite so useless, as doing with great efficiency, something that should not be done at all."

Peter F. Drucker

List three activities that you perform on a regular basis, with great efficiency, that do not provide value or help you to move your goals forward:

1. _____
   _____

2. _____
   _____

3. _____
   _____

Name at least three other people who can perform those tasks for you?

1. _____
2. _____
3. _____

Six Months Review:

_____
_____
_____

Quotation Source Information:

_____
_____
_____

January 9
July 10

"The liberally educated person is one who is able to resist the easy and preferred answers, not because he is obstinate but because he knows others worthy of consideration."

Allan Bloom

Describe what you can do to ensure that your business and systems analysis is innovative and creative; and does not accept the easy answers:

_____
_____
_____
_____
_____

Six Months Review:

_____
_____
_____

Quotation Source Information:

_____
_____
_____

January 10
July 11

"The propensity to truck, barter and exchange one
thing for another ... is common to all men,
and to be found in no other race of animals."

Adam Smith

As system professionals you will be required to manage the negotiation
of many different types of contracts and arrangements. Describe how
you will develop and improve your negotiating technique.

_____
_____
_____
_____
_____

Name three people who you will help to become better negotiators.
Contact them for a meeting to accomplish this goal.

1. _____
2. _____
3. _____

Six Months Review:

_____
_____
_____

Quotation Source Information:

_____
_____
_____

January 11
July 12

"You have not converted a man because
you have silenced him."

John Morley

Describe a situation when you thought that your developers or business partners agreed with your solution because they did not say anything.

_____
_____
_____
_____
_____

What will you do to ensure that all ideas are being considered in your systems solution?

_____
_____
_____
_____
_____

Six Months Review:

_____
_____
_____

Quotation Source Information:

_____
_____
_____

January 12
July 13

"The average home today contains more computing power than all of NASA did when John Glenn made that first flight 36 years ago."

Vice President Al Gore

How will you make certain that you are helping your company to stay current with technology?

_____
_____
_____
_____
_____

How will you keep yourself current with the changes in technology?

_____
_____
_____
_____
_____

Six Months Review:

_____
_____
_____

Quotation Source Information:

_____
_____
_____

January 13
July 14

"There are only two ways to live your life.
One is as though nothing is a miracle.
The other is as though everything is a miracle."

Albert Einstein

Often your business partners will view your systems solutions to complex business problems as miracles. However, sometimes the solution can be as simple as modifying the business process and does not require a technology solution.

What can you do to make sure that each business problem is resolved with the simplest solution?

1. _____
   _____

2. _____
   _____

3. _____
   _____

Six Months Review:
_____
_____
_____

Quotation Source Information:
_____
_____
_____

January 14
July 15

"Technological progress has merely provided us with more efficient means for going backwards."

Aldous Huxley

What do you do to guarantee that your systems solutions are not automating inefficient processes?

_____

_____

_____

_____

_____

Six Months Review:

_____

_____

_____

Quotation Source Information:

_____

_____

_____

January 15
July 16

"The job of an IT professional is to create
the future vision for your company to use
information technology as a competitive weapon."

Wayne L. Anderson

What is your technology vision for your company?

_____
_____
_____

List the top three activities that you will perform today to move towards your vision and help your company to use technology as a strategic weapon:

1. _____
   _____

2. _____
   _____

3. _____
   _____

Six Months Review:

_____
_____
_____

Quotation Source Information:

_____
_____
_____

January 16
July 17

"The production of too many useful things results in too many useless people."

Karl Marx

What procedures will you develop to account for the people who may be displaced by the systems that you implement?

1. _____
   _____

2. _____
   _____

3. _____
   _____

How can you share your techniques with other systems developers?

_____
_____
_____

Six Months Review:

_____
_____
_____

Quotation Source Information:

_____
_____
_____

January 17
July 18

"All styles are good except the tiresome kind."

Voltaire

Is your management style *tiresome*? List three things that you will do today to energize your management style.

1. _____
   _____

2. _____
   _____

3. _____
   _____

Six Months Review:
_____
_____
_____

Quotation Source Information:
_____
_____
_____

January 18
July 19

"Do not go where the path may lead,
go instead where there is no path and leave a trail."

Ralph Waldo Emerson

What will you do today to help your company to utilize information technology to create a path in the marketplace that does not currently exist?

_____
_____
_____
_____
_____

How will you implement your strategy?

_____
_____
_____
_____
_____

Six Months Review:

_____
_____
_____

Quotation Source Information:

_____
_____
_____

January 19
July 20

"Diligence is the mother of good luck."

Benjamin Franklin

What are the top three scenarios that get in the way of you being diligent in your pursuit of sound information technology solutions?

1. _____
   _____

2. _____
   _____

3. _____
   _____

What will you do today to eliminate those obstacles and create your own luck?

_____
_____
_____
_____
_____

Six Months Review:

_____
_____
_____

Quotation Source Information:

_____
_____
_____

January 20
July 21

"I love deadlines. I love the whooshing sound they make as they fly by."

Douglas Adams

What will you do to improve on the delivery times of your information system projects?

_____

_____

_____

_____

_____

List some ways you can help your subordinates (or teammates) to deliver information system solutions on time:

1. _____

_____

2. _____

_____

3. _____

_____

Six Months Review:

_____

_____

_____

Quotation Source Information:

_____

_____

_____

January 21
July 22

"Always listen to experts.
They'll tell you what can't be done and why.
Then do it."

Robert A. Heinlein

Information system professionals are always challenged with doing what other people don't think can be done. However, some problems are so complex that they require input from many different people. List the steps you will use to analyze and determine which advice to use and which advice you will eliminate:

1. _____
2. _____
3. _____
4. _____
5. _____
6. _____
7. _____
8. _____
9. _____
10. _____

Six Months Review:

_____
_____
_____

Quotation Source Information:

_____
_____
_____

January 22
July 23

"If you fail to plan, you plan to fail by default"

Tariq Siddique

IT Professionals are usually required to manage a large number of complicated tasks simultaneously. The professionals who are successful are the ones that have a good set of detailed plans for each task. Describe the steps that are necessary to create a good set of plans:

1. _____
2. _____
3. _____
4. _____
5. _____

Name three people who are exceptionally good at creating plans. Contact those people and learn their secrets.

1. _____
2. _____
3. _____

Six Months Review:

_____
_____
_____

Quotation Source Information:

_____
_____
_____

January 23
July 24

"If computers get too powerful, we can organize them into a committee—that will do them in."

Bradley's Bromide

How will you go about minimizing the number of unproductive committees in which you participate?

1. _____

   _____

2. _____

   _____

3. _____

   _____

How will you teach others to follow these steps as well?

_____

_____

_____

Six Months Review:

_____

_____

_____

Quotation Source Information:

_____

_____

_____

January 24
July 25

> "In a hierarchy, every employee tends to
> rise to his level of incompetence."

Dr. Laurence J. Peter

What will you do to keep from reaching your level of incompetence?

1. _____
   _____

2. _____
   _____

3. _____
   _____

4. _____
   _____

5. _____
   _____

How do you pass those lessons onto other IT professionals?

_____
_____
_____

Six Months Review:

_____
_____
_____

Quotation Source Information:

_____
_____
_____

January 25
July 26

"There is only one thing that frustrates me about computers—everything!"

Peter Biadasz

List three things that frustrate you or your business partners about the computer systems that in use:

1. _____
   _____

2. _____
   _____

3. _____
   _____

Document the things you will begin to do today that will improve their situation.

_____
_____
_____
_____
_____

Six Months Review:

_____
_____
_____

Quotation Source Information:

_____

_____

_____

January 26
July 27

"A definition of insanity: doing the same thing over and over again in the same way and expecting different results."

Rita Mae Brown

Systems professionals are required to be innovative. You are required to constantly develop new ideas, create solutions to complex problems and creatively improve the business process. How do you go about being innovative?

_____

_____

_____

How do will you teach others to be innovative?

_____

_____

_____

Who are the most creative people that you know? List the behaviors that make them innovative:

_____

_____

_____

Six Months Review:

_____

_____

_____

Quotation Source Information:

_____

_____

_____

January 27
July 28

> "So much of what we call management consists
> in making it difficult for people to work."

Peter F. Drucker

What steps will you take to make certain that it is easy for the people that you manage to get their work done?

1. _____
   _____

2. _____
   _____

3. _____
   _____

How will you avoid micro-managing your team of IT professionals?

_____
_____
_____

Six Months Review:

_____
_____
_____

Quotation Source Information:

_____
_____
_____

January 28
July 29

"Do not be bullied out of your common sense by the specialist; two to one, he is a pedant."

Oliver Wendell Holmes

Most systems professionals are specialists. This generally means they are very good at what they do. However, sometimes simple common sense should prevail. List the top three specialists that you know and respect:

1. _____
   _____

2. _____
   _____

3. _____
   _____

How will you handle advice that you receive from specialist if you think a common sense approach is more appropriate?

_____
_____
_____
_____
_____

Six Months Review:

_____
_____
_____

Quotation Source Information:

_____

_____

_____

January 29
July 30

"Technology makes it possible for people to gain control over everything, except over technology."

John Tudor

How do you keep from implementing technology for technology sake?

_____

_____

_____

What will you do to make sure that the technology is consistent with the direction of the company?

_____

_____

_____

How will you teach other systems professionals to manage the implementation of technology?

_____

_____

_____

Six Months Review:

_____

_____

_____

Quotation Source Information:

_____

_____

_____

January 30
July 31

"Too many people are like wheelbarrows—
useful only when pushed and too easily upset."

Unknown

It is essential that IT professionals be self-motivated. How do you go about motivating yourself so that you don't require a *push* to get started?

1. _____
   _____

2. _____
   _____

3. _____
   _____

Not every idea that you present will be accepted. What do you do to manage your emotions so that you are not easily upset?

_____
_____
_____

Six Months Review:

_____
_____
_____

January 31
August 1

"I do not seek, I find."

Pablo Picasso

Do you spend your time searching for the perfect technology or are you finding different and unique ways to implement the technology that you have?

Select three different technologies that you currently have in your company that you have control over its use:

1. _____

2. _____

3. _____

Describe a unique way in which you will use each of those technologies to bring additional value to your company:

_____
_____
_____
_____
_____

Six Months Review:

_____
_____
_____

Quotation Source Information:

_____
_____
_____

February 1
August 2

"Chance favors the prepared mind."

Louis Pasteur

What are some ways that you can prepare yourself to achieve your professional goals?

1. _____
   _____

2. _____
   _____

3. _____
   _____

4. _____
   _____

How will you prepare your mind so that you will increase the probability of chance favoring you?

_____
_____
_____

Six Months Review:

_____
_____
_____

Quotation Source Information:

_____
_____
_____

February 2
August 3

"It has become appallingly obvious that our technology has exceeded our humanity."

Albert Einstein

Technology solutions can sometimes ignore the needs of the people using it. How will you ensure that the technology that you implement will consider the needs of its users?

_____
_____
_____
_____
_____

What steps will you take to educate your systems developers about creating user-friendly systems?

_____
_____
_____
_____
_____

Six Months Review:

_____
_____
_____

Quotation Source Information:

_____
_____
_____

February 3
August 4

"Not one of the things that you have done to date, will mean anything if you don't deliver."

Wayne L. Anderson

The way that an IT professional can bring value to a company is to deliver the systems products to the business when it is needed and at the agreed upon cost. List the steps that you take to deliver your products on time:

_____
_____
_____
_____
_____

Contact the systems professionals that you consider exceptional at delivering system products on time. What do they do that makes them successful?

_____
_____
_____

Six Months Review:

_____
_____
_____

Quotation Source Information:

_____
_____
_____

February 4
August 5

"The nice thing about standards is
that there are so many of them to choose from."

Andrew S. Tanenbaum

What process will you use to select the appropriate standards for your
IT organization?

1. _____
   _____

2. _____
   _____

3. _____
   _____

Six Months Review:

_____
_____
_____

Quotation Source Information:

_____
_____
_____

February 5
August 6

"IT—you can't live with it and you can't live without it."

Vanposetski

Describe a critical application that is used by your primary internal customer that is clear that they dislike using.

_____
_____
_____
_____
_____

List three things that you can do today that could improve their experience with the aforementioned system.

1. _____
   _____

2. _____
   _____

3. _____
   _____

Six Months Review:

_____
_____
_____

Quotation Source Information:

_____

_____

_____

February 6
August 7

> "I have not failed. I have found 10,000 ways
> that won't work."

Thomas A. Edison

How do you determine whether or not your endeavor will succeed?

_____
_____
_____
_____
_____

What do you do to keep moving forward so that new ideas may surface?

_____
_____
_____
_____
_____

Six Months Review:

_____
_____
_____

Quotation Source Information:

_____
_____
_____

February 7
August 8

"All truths are easy to understand once they are
discovered; the point is to discover them."

Galileo Galilei

It is essential for systems professionals to uncover how business
processes really work in order for you to find appropriate solutions. This
does not always happen by just asking people. How do you discover the
truth about how things really work?

1. _____
   _____

2. _____
   _____

3. _____
   _____

4. _____
   _____

Six Months Review:
_____
_____
_____

Quotation Source Information:
_____
_____
_____

February 8
August 9

> "Experience enables you to recognize a mistake
> when you make it again."

Franklin P. Jones

When a systems professional makes a mistake it generally costs the company a great deal of money. What do you do to learn from your mistakes so that they are not repeated?

1. _____
   _____

2. _____
   _____

3. _____
   _____

How do you teach other IT professionals to do the same?

_____
_____
_____

Six Months Review:

_____
_____
_____

Quotation Source Information:

_____
_____
_____

February 9
August 10

> "Being defeated is often a temporary condition.
> Giving up is what makes it permanent."

Marlene vos Savant

Systems solutions don't always go as planned. How do you handle defeat?

_____
_____
_____

What steps do you take to continue to make progress?

1. _____
   _____

2. _____
   _____

3. _____
   _____

Six Months Review:

_____
_____
_____

Quotation Source Information:

_____
_____
_____

February 10
August 11

"The reverse side also has a reverse side."

Japanese Proverb

Generally, there are many alternatives and approaches to solving a business problem using technology. What steps do you take to review all sides of the possible solutions?

1. _____

2. _____

3. _____

Who do you know that is good at researching alternatives and what do they do?

1. _____

2. _____

3. _____

Six Months Review:

_____
_____
_____

Quotation Source Information:

_____
_____
_____

February 11
August 12

> "Everyone thinks of changing the world,
> but no one thinks of changing themselves."

Leo Tolstoy

Your job as a system professional is to be a change agent. You are requested on a daily basis to change business processes and as a result, change the lives of many people. What do you do to change and improve your own professional life?

_____
_____
_____
_____
_____

What will you do today?

_____
_____
_____
_____
_____

Six Months Review:

_____
_____
_____

Quotation Source Information:

_____
_____
_____

February 12
August 13

"You can't build a reputation on what you are going to do."

Henry Ford

Describe the reputation that you have for getting things done.

_____
_____
_____
_____
_____

What will you do to improve that reputation?

_____
_____
_____
_____

Six Months Review:

_____
_____
_____

Quotation Source Information:

_____
_____
_____

February 13
August 14

"Obstacles are those frightening things you see when you take our eyes off of the goal."

Hannah More

What steps do you take to ensure that you keep your eye on your professional goals?

1. _____
   _____

2. _____
   _____

3. _____
   _____

What do you do when you run into an obstacle?

_____
_____
_____

Six Months Review:

_____
_____
_____

Quotation Source Information:

_____
_____
_____

February 14
August 15

"We find comfort among those who agree with us
—growth among those who don't."

Frank A. Clark

What steps do you take to solicit ideas from people who may not be in total agreement with you?

1. _____
   _____

2. _____
   _____

3. _____
   _____

Who do you know that is a master at requesting ideas from different people? What techniques do they use?

_____
_____
_____

Six Months Review:

_____
_____
_____

Quotation Source Information:

_____
_____
_____

February 15
August 16

> "As a tool, computer applications are limitless;
> it is my mind that is limited."

Peter Biadasz

What personal steps do you take to motivate yourself during a time when it is not particularly comfortable to do so?

1. _____
   _____

2. _____
   _____

3. _____
   _____

Discuss this topic with a person who you think is extremely good at self-motivation. Learn what they do.

_____
_____
_____

Six Months Review:

_____
_____
_____

Quotation Source Information:

_____
_____
_____

February 16
August 17

"Computers make it easier to do a lot of things, but most of the things they make it easier to do don't need to be done."

Andy Rooney

It is imperative, that as a good systems professional, you must develop valuable, productive systems. Describe the process you follow to develop systems that provide value to the company.

_____
_____
_____
_____
_____

Six Months Review:

_____
_____
_____

Quotation Source Information:

_____
_____
_____

February 17
August 18

> "The best thing about the future is that
> it comes one day at a time."

Abraham Lincoln

Describe how you make certain that each day is progressing toward your business and professional goals:

_____
_____
_____
_____
_____

What message is Abraham Lincoln giving us in this quote?

_____
_____
_____

Six Months Review:

_____
_____
_____

Quotation Source Information:

_____
_____
_____

February 18
August 19

> "In a few minutes a computer can make a mistake
> so great that it would have taken
> many men many months to equal it."

Unknown

List the procedure that you use to provide quality assurance to the business and system processes that you implement:

1. _____
2. _____
3. _____
4. _____
5. _____

What will you do to improve those procedures?

_____
_____
_____

Six Months Review:

_____
_____
_____

February 19
August 20

"Aim for the top. There is plenty of room there.
There are so few at the top it is almost lonely there."

Samuel Insull

List your top three professional goals:

1. _____
_____

2. _____
_____

3. _____
_____

Talk with two people who has attained each of those goals and describe
how they techniques they used to achieve them.

_____
_____
_____
_____
_____

Six Months Review:

_____
_____
_____

Quotation Source Information:

_____
_____
_____

February 20
August 21

"To avoid criticism, do nothing, say nothing and be nothing."

Elbert Hubbard

Describe a situation when the primary reason for your actions was to avoid being visible:

_____

_____

_____

_____

Identify three people that you think are very visible regardless of the amount of criticism they receive.

1. _____

_____

2. _____

_____

3. _____

_____

Describe the things that you can learn from what they do:

_____

_____

_____

Six Months Review:

_____

_____

_____

Quotation Source Information:

_____

_____

_____

February 21
August 22

"You will never find time for anything. If you want time, you must make it."

Charles Bixton

List three things that get in the way of your ability to make progress.

1. _____
_____

2. _____
_____

3. _____
_____

What time management techniques will you employ in order to keep those items from impeding your progress?

_____
_____
_____

Six Months Review:

_____
_____
_____

Quotation Source Information:

_____
_____
_____

February 22
August 23

"Be not simply good—be good for something."

Henry David Thoreau

Are you just a good system professional? Describe how you think your business partners, superior and peers perceive your value.

_____
_____
_____
_____
_____

Contact one person from each type listed above and validate your perceptions.

_____
_____
_____

Six Months Review:

_____
_____
_____

Quotation Source Information:

_____
_____
_____

February 23
August 24

"Don't tell people how to do things, tell them what to do and let them surprise you with their results."

George S. Patton

How does your management technique differ from the above quote?

_____
_____
_____

What steps will you take to improve your people management style?

1. _____
2. _____
3. _____

Six Months Review:

_____
_____
_____

Quotation Source Information:

_____
_____
_____

February 24
August 25

"The only test of leadership is that somebody follows."

Robert K. Greenleaf

List three reasons why other IT professionals should follow you:

1. _____
   _____

2. _____
   _____

3. _____
   _____

Describe three ways that you can improve your leadership skills:

1. _____
   _____

2. _____
   _____

3. _____
   _____

Six Months Review:

_____
_____
_____

Quotation Source Information:

_____

_____

_____

February 25
August 26

"Any sufficiently advanced technology is indistinguishable from magic."

Arthur C. Clarke

Describe how you educate your business partners about how technology works so that it doesn't appear to be magic.

_____
_____
_____
_____
_____

Six Months Review:

_____
_____
_____

Quotation Source Information:

_____
_____
_____

February 26
August 27

> "I conceive that knowledge of books is the basis on which all other knowledge rests."

George Washington

List at least three books that you will read to improve your business knowledge:

1. _____

2. _____

3. _____

List at least three books that you will read to improve your information technology knowledge:

1. _____

2. _____

3. _____

Six Months Review:

_____

_____

_____

Quotation Source Information:

_____
_____
_____

February 27
August 28

"I recommend you to take care of the minutes,
for the hours will take care of themselves."

Lord Chesterfield

What is the meaning of Lord Chesterfield's quote?

_____
_____
_____
_____
_____

How does the Lord Chesterfield quote apply to system development projects?

_____
_____
_____
_____
_____

Six Months Review:

_____
_____
_____

Quotation Source Information:

_____
_____
_____

February 28
August 29

"Strong ethical behavior is good business."

Wayne L. Anderson

Systems professionals have many opportunities to compromise their ethics by the mere nature of their work. You are exposed to a great deal of sensitive information that is necessary to complete your assignments. What steps do you take to ensure that you personally maintain strong ethical behavior?

_____
_____
_____

Who are the most ethical people that you know? List the behaviors and traits that make them strong ethical people:

1. _____
2. _____
3. _____
4. _____
5. _____

Six Months Review:

_____
_____
_____

Quotation Source Information:

_____
_____
_____

February 29
August 30

"The purchasing agent faces the toughest decision when he negotiates to buy the machine designed to replace him."

Unknown

It is common for a businessperson to assist an IT professional in designing and implementing a system that will ultimately replace that businessperson. Describe how you work with a businessperson who in this position:

_____
_____
_____
_____
_____

How will you teach others to work with and be sensitive to the business professionals that are in this situation?

_____
_____
_____
_____

Six Months Review:

_____
_____
_____

March 1
August 31

"Silence is the ultimate weapon of power."

Charles de Gaulle

Describe a situation where you could have been victorious had you remained silent:

_____
_____
_____
_____
_____

What did you learn?

_____
_____
_____
_____
_____

Six Months Review:

_____
_____
_____

Quotation Source Information:

_____
_____
_____

March 2
September 1

"Things should be made as simple as possible, but no simpler."

Albert Einstein

Describe the method that you use to ensure that your system solutions are as simple as possible:

_____
_____
_____
_____
_____

What are the top three things that you can teach other system professionals to do that will make their implementations simple?

1. _____
_____

2. _____
_____

3. _____
_____

Six Months Review:

_____
_____
_____

Quotation Source Information:

_____
_____
_____

March 3
September 2

"No problem can withstand the assault
of sustained thinking."

Voltaire

System professionals are solution providers. You are expected to overcome problems and present workable solutions that provide value to your company. List the steps that you will follow to attack and resolve problems:

1. _____
2. _____
3. _____
4. _____
5. _____

Six Months Review:

_____
_____
_____

Quotation Source Information:

_____
_____
_____

March 4
September 3

> "I am always doing that which I can not do,
> in order that I may learn how to do it."

Pablo Picasso

Describe a time when you operated *outside of the box* and did things that you did not know how to do or use technology that you never used before:

_____
_____
_____
_____
_____

List three things that you learned from the experience:

1. _____
   _____

2. _____
   _____

3. _____
   _____

Six Months Review:

_____
_____
_____

Quotation Source Information:

_____
_____
_____

March 5
September 4

"Information technology has been with us since the beginning of time. It just happened to hit warp speed in the 20th Century."

POZ

What do you think is the most significant development in information technology in the 20th century?

_____
_____
_____
_____
_____

What can you do to convert those developments into a strategic weapon for your company?

_____
_____
_____
_____
_____

Six Months Review:

_____
_____
_____

Quotation Source Information:

_____
_____
_____

March 6
September 5

> "Management is doing things right;
> leadership is doing the right things."

Peter F. Drucker

List three other traits of a good leader:

1. _____
   _____

2. _____
   _____

3. _____
   _____

Contact two people who you think are exceptional leaders and learn what they think are good leadership traits.

_____
_____
_____

Six Months Review:

_____
_____
_____

Quotation Source Information:

_____
_____
_____

March 7
September 6

> "A habit cannot be tossed out the window;
> it must be coaxed down the stairs a step at a time."

Mark Twain

What are the top three habits that would make you a better system professional if you were to eliminate them?

1. _____
   _____

2. _____
   _____

3. _____
   _____

Determine the steps that you will take to eliminate each one on your list.

_____
_____
_____

Six Months Review:

_____
_____
_____

Quotation Source Information:

_____
_____
_____

March 8
September 7

"Goals create focus."

Unknown

List ways in which your information technology goals help to create focus for your company:

1. _____
   _____

2. _____
   _____

3. _____
   _____

Six Months Review:

_____
_____
_____

March 9
September 8

"If it's a good idea, go ahead and do it. It is much easier to apologize than it is to get permission."

Admiral Grace Hopper

List at least three good ideas that you have *not* acted upon because you believe you needed to have permission to begin:

1. _____
   _____

2. _____
   _____

3. _____
   _____

Select at least one idea from the list that you will begin to work on **TODAY!**

Six Months Review:
_____
_____
_____

Quotation Source Information:
_____
_____
_____

March 10
September 9

"If you are too busy to help those around you
succeed, you're too busy."

Unknown

List five things that you will do today to help one of your teammates to
succeed:

1. _____
   _____

2. _____
   _____

3. _____
   _____

4. _____
   _____

5. _____
   _____

Six Months Review:

_____
_____
_____

March 11
September 10

"The difference between ordinary and extraordinary is that little extra."

Zig Ziglar

List three things that you will do today that will be over and above your normal duties:

1. _____
   _____

2. _____
   _____

3. _____
   _____

Six Months Review:
_____
_____
_____

Quotation Source Information:
_____
_____
_____

March 12
September 11

"Americans still care about quality. The country is full of intelligent, courageous people who would change if they only knew how."

W. Edward Deming

List the steps that you follow to improve the quality of your product:

1. _____

2. _____

3. _____

4. _____

5. _____

Name three people who you think needs the quality of their product improved. Contact each of them today and teach them your process.

1. _____
2. _____
3. _____

Six Months Review:

_____
_____
_____

Quotation Source Information:

_____

_____

_____

March 13
September 12

"Politics are almost as exciting as war, and quite as dangerous. In war you can only be killed once, but in politics many times."

Winston Churchill

IT professionals tend to avoid and/or ignore the politics that exist within their companies. However, success in many companies is based on an individual's ability to operate within the company's political structure.

What do you plan to do today to begin to understand the political structure and process within your company?

_____
_____
_____
_____
_____

Who can you contact to help you to understand the political structure and process?

_____
_____
_____
_____
_____

Six Months Review:

_____
_____
_____

Quotation Source Information:

_____

_____

_____

March 14
September 13

"All activity isn't progress,
just like all movement isn't forward."

Wayne L. Anderson

List the top five unproductive activities that you perform:

1. _____
2. _____
3. _____
4. _____
5. _____

Document what you are going to do to eliminate those activities:

_____
_____
_____
_____
_____

Six Months Review:

_____
_____
_____

Quotation Source Information:

_____
_____
_____

March 15
September 14

"Why, after years of me studying computers, do my children know more about computers than I?"

Peter Biadasz

It is the job of every system professional to stay abreast of information technology developments. Unfortunately, however, this is not the case for most the people for whom you are developing systems. Describe the best way to keep your business partners up-to-date with the changes in information technology:

_____
_____
_____
_____
_____

Six Months Review:

_____
_____
_____

Quotation Source Information:

_____
_____
_____

March 16
September 15

"Try not to become a man of success
but rather try to become a man of value."

Albert Einstein

List your top five values:

1. _____
_____

2. _____
_____

3. _____
_____

4. _____
_____

5. _____
_____

Six Months Review:

_____
_____
_____

Quotation Source Information:

_____
_____
_____

March 17
September 16

"Farming looks mighty easy when your plow
is a pencil and you're a thousand miles
from the corn field."

Dwight D. Eisenhower

When you are designing a systems solution, what steps do you take to understand your business partner's problem?

1. _____
   _____

2. _____
   _____

3. _____
   _____

4. _____
   _____

5. _____
   _____

Six Months Review:
_____
_____
_____

Quotation Source Information:
_____
_____
_____

March 18
September 17

> "Failure is only the opportunity to begin
> again more intelligently."

Henry Ford

List the last three situations where you believe you failed:

1. _____

2. _____

3. _____

Describe the lesson that you learned from each.

1. _____

2. _____

3. _____

What will you change today in order to be more successful in the future?

_____
_____
_____

Six Months Review:

_____
_____
_____

Quotation Source Information:

_____
_____
_____

March 19
September 18

"There are three things extremely hard: steel,
a diamond and to know one's self."

Benjamin Franklin

How do you go about learning yourself?

_____

_____

_____

Contact five people that you trust and ask them to describe you. What are the three things that you heard that surprised you? If nothing surprised you, then ask five more people. Continue the process until you have learned three new things about the way other people see you.

1. _____

2. _____

3. _____

4. _____

5. _____

Six Months Review:

_____

_____

_____

Quotation Source Information:

_____

_____

_____

March 20
September 19

> "The weak can never forgive.
> Forgiveness is the attribute of the strong."
>
> **Mahatma Gandhi**

List three people that you need to forgive:

1. _____
   _____

2. _____
   _____

3. _____
   _____

Describe how you plan to approach them.

_____
_____
_____

Contact each of those people today and forgive them.

Six Months Review:

_____
_____
_____

Quotation Source Information:

_____
_____
_____

March 21
September 20

"The most valuable of all talents is that of never using two words when one will do."

Thomas Jefferson

List three situations where you would have been more successful had you used one word instead of two:

1. _____
   _____

2. _____
   _____

3. _____
   _____

What will you do today to improve on your ability to get your point across with fewer words?

_____
_____
_____

Six Months Review:

_____
_____
_____

Quotation Source Information:

_____
_____
_____

March 22
September 21

"The system of nature, of which man is a part, tends
to be self-balancing, self-adjusting, self-cleansing.
Not so with technology."

E.F. Schumacher

Describe how your systems development processes will result in systems
that are self-balancing, self-adjusting, and self-cleansing (i.e. self-correcting):

_____
_____
_____
_____
_____

Six Months Review:

_____
_____
_____

Quotation Source Information:

_____
_____
_____

March 23
September 22

> "Let us never negotiate out of fear but
> let us never fear to negotiate."

John F. Kennedy

IT professionals must negotiate on a regular basis. What was your most difficult negotiating situation?

_____
_____
_____
_____
_____

What do you plan to do to improve your negotiating skills?

_____
_____
_____
_____
_____

Six Months Review:

_____
_____
_____

Quotation Source Information:

_____
_____
_____

March 24
September 23

"We must use time creatively—and forever realize that the time is always hope to do great things."

Martin Luther King, Jr.

List three people that you know that have exceptional time management techniques:

1. _____
   _____

2. _____
   _____

3. _____
   _____

Contact each of them today and learn at least one technique from each of them.

_____
_____
_____
_____
_____

Six Months Review:

_____
_____
_____

Quotation Source Information:

_____

_____

_____

March 25
September 24

"Am I not destroying my enemies when I make friends of them?"

Abraham Lincoln

List three people with whom you have been having a difficult time:

1. _____
   _____

2. _____
   _____

3. _____
   _____

Develop a plan to make them your friends:

_____
_____
_____
_____
_____

Begin executing your plan today!

Six Months Review:

_____
_____
_____

Quotation Source Information:

_____

_____

_____

March 26
September 25

"The quality of a person's life is in direct proportion to their commitment to excellence, regardless of their chosen field of endeavor."

Vince Lombardi

Who are the people who you think are vigorously committed to excellence?

1. _____
   _____

2. _____
   _____

3. _____
   _____

Describe what they do that is different than what you do:

_____
_____
_____
_____
_____

Six Months Review:

_____
_____
_____

Quotation Source Information:

_____

_____

_____

March 27
September 26

"Old age is like a plane flying through a storm. Once
you're aboard, there's nothing you can do."

Golda Meir

What activities will you do to preserve your youth?

_____
_____
_____
_____
_____

Name three people who are good at maintaining a youthful attitude.

1. _____

2. _____

3. _____

What do they do?

_____
_____
_____
_____
_____

Six Months Review:

_____
_____
_____

Quotation Source Information:

_____

_____

_____

March 28
September 27

> "The most vital quality a soldier can possess
> is self-confidence."

George S. Patton

Describe your feelings about your own self-confidence:

_____
_____
_____
_____
_____

What will you do today to begin to improve your self-confidence?

_____
_____
_____
_____
_____

Six Months Review:

_____
_____
_____

Quotation Source Information:

_____
_____
_____

March 29
September 28

"Never before have we had so little time
in which to do so much."

Franklin D. Roosevelt

Systems professionals seem to always be given tasks that require more time than is usually allotted. Name three people who always seem to have enough time to get things done:

1. _____
   _____

2. _____
   _____

3. _____
   _____

What do they do to accomplish their tasks that are different from what you do?

_____
_____
_____
_____
_____

Six Months Review:

_____
_____
_____

Quotation Source Information:

_____

_____

_____

March 30
September 29

"A good idea doesn't care who produces it ...
and neither should you."

Wayne L. Anderson

How do you take an idea and turn them into action regardless of who produces it?

1. _____

_____

2. _____

_____

3. _____

_____

How will you teach others to accept and act on good ideas?

_____
_____
_____
_____
_____

Six Months Review:

_____
_____
_____

Quotation Source Information:

_____
_____
_____

March 31
September 30

"The best executive is the one who has sense enough
to pick good men to do what he wants done and
self-restraint enough to keep from meddling with
them while they do it."

Theodore Roosevelt

Name three managers you know that are experts at *not* micro-managing
their people:

1. _____
   _____

2. _____
   _____

3. _____
   _____

Contact each of them and document at least one thing that you can
learn from each that will improve your management style.

_____
_____
_____
_____
_____

Six Months Review:

_____
_____
_____

Quotation Source Information:

_____

_____

_____

April 1
October 1

"Most computer users don't care about the details
involved with computers; they just want them to
work, just like the phone and the light switch."

Peter Biadasz

The business people who you work with each day perform functions
such as marketing, finance, product development, etc. Information
technology is not the primary thing on their mind. Therefore, they view
the inner workings of computer systems as a utility similar to their
telephones and the lights in their offices.

What can you do to ensure that your business partners do not have to
worry about the internal workings of their computer?

———————————————————————————
———————————————————————————
———————————————————————————
———————————————————————————
———————————————————————————

Six Months Review:

———————————————————————————
———————————————————————————
———————————————————————————

Quotation Source Information:

———————————————————————————
———————————————————————————
———————————————————————————

April 2
October 2

> "I usually make up my mind about a man in ten seconds, and I very rarely change it."

Margaret Thatcher

If someone made up their mind about you in ten seconds, what would be their description of you?

_____
_____
_____
_____
_____

What would you change to improve that description?

_____
_____
_____
_____
_____

Six Months Review:

_____
_____
_____

Quotation Source Information:

_____
_____
_____

April 3
October 3

"Being a president is like riding a tiger.
A man has to keep on riding or he is swallowed."

Harry S. Truman

Describe how this quote also applies to being an IT professional:

_____
_____
_____
_____
_____

What will you do to keep *riding* and successfully achieve your endeavors?

_____
_____
_____
_____
_____

Six Months Review:

_____
_____
_____

Quotation Source Information:

_____
_____
_____

April 4
October 4

"Excellence is to do a common thing
in an uncommon way."

Booker T. Washington

Based on the above quote, describe a situation where you have demonstrated excellence in your undertakings:

_____
_____
_____
_____
_____

What will you do to improve your ability to do a common thing in an uncommon way?

_____
_____
_____
_____
_____

Six Months Review:

_____
_____
_____

Quotation Source Information:

_____
_____
_____

April 5
October 5

"Humanity has been propelled forward by the eye glass, the printing press and information technology."

Richard Possett

List some ways that you have used technology to propel your company forward:

1. _____
   _____

2. _____
   _____

3. _____
   _____

Six Months Review:

_____
_____
_____

Quotation Source Information:

_____
_____
_____

April 6
October 6

> "Do not let what you cannot do interfere
> with what you can do."

John Wooden

List three things areas in which you would like to improve yourself:

1. _____
   _____

2. _____
   _____

3. _____
   _____

Describe how improving those areas will allow you to achieve your goals:

_____
_____
_____
_____
_____

Six Months Review:

_____
_____
_____

Quotation Source Information:

_____
_____
_____

April 7
October 7

"There is no success without hardship."

Sophocles

What hardship have you experienced while attempting to achieve your goal?

_____
_____
_____
_____
_____

What did you learn from the experience?

_____
_____
_____
_____
_____

Six Months Review:

_____
_____
_____

Quotation Source Information:

_____
_____
_____

April 8
October 8

"All things are difficult before they are easy."

Thomas Fuller

As an IT professional, what is the one task that you find the most difficult?

_____
_____
_____
_____
_____

Describe your plan to make that task easy:

_____
_____
_____
_____
_____

Six Months Review:

_____
_____
_____

Quotation Source Information:

_____
_____
_____

April 9
October 9

"I have learned that success is to be measured
not so much by the position that one has reached
in life as by the obstacles which he has overcome
while trying to succeed."

Booker T. Washington

What is the main obstacle that is getting in the way of your success?

_____
_____
_____

List three people that you know that have faced the same obstacle:

_____
_____
_____

Contact each person and learn how he or she overcame that obstacle.

_____
_____
_____

Now, do the same thing that they did!

Six Months Review:

_____
_____
_____

Quotation Source Information:

_____

_____

_____

April 10
October 10

"People with goals succeed
because they know where they're going."

Earl Nightingale

Review the progress that you have made on your goals to-date.

_____
_____
_____
_____
_____

What adjustments will you make to ensure that you achieve those goals?

_____
_____
_____
_____
_____

Six Months Review:

_____
_____
_____

Quotation Source Information:

_____
_____
_____

April 11
October 11

"Nothing happens unless first a dream."

Carl Sandburg

What is your dream?

_____
_____
_____
_____
_____

What will you do today to make progress toward that dream?

_____
_____
_____
_____
_____

Six Months Review:

_____
_____
_____

Quotation Source Information:

_____
_____
_____

April 12
October 12

"Every great and commanding moment in the annals of the world is the triumph of some enthusiasm."

Ralph Waldo Emerson

A successful systems professional sees to always have enthusiasm about what they are doing. Describe your level of enthusiasm about your work:

_____
_____
_____
_____
_____

What will you do today to improve your level of enthusiasm?

_____
_____
_____
_____
_____

Six Months Review:

_____
_____
_____

Quotation Source Information:

_____
_____
_____

April 13
October 13

"A good plan is like a road map: it shows the
final destination and usually marks the best way to
get there …"

H. Stanley Judd

Describe where you are going in your career in terms of the end
destination:

_____
_____
_____
_____
_____

List the path you are taking to achieve your final career goal:

1. _____

2. _____

3. _____

4. _____

5. _____

Six Months Review:

_____
_____
_____

Quotation Source Information:

_____

_____

_____

April 14
October 14

"What kills a skunk is the publicity it gives itself."

Abraham Lincoln

What three things will you do today to be more humble?

1. _____
   _____

2. _____
   _____

3. _____
   _____

Six Months Review:
_____
_____
_____

Quotation Source Information:
_____
_____
_____

April 15
October 15

"No meaningful aim will ever be attained if all possible objections must first be overcome."

Wayne L. Anderson

There are a great number of people who want every detail to be thoroughly investigated and analyzed before they begin to move forward. This has a tendency to paralyze people to a point where nothing meaningful gets accomplished.

Describe what steps you are going to take to ensure that you are always moving forward:

_____
_____
_____
_____
_____

Identify two people who can help you to determine the *right* amount of analysis before moving forward:

1. _____
   _____

2. _____
   _____

Six Months Review:

_____
_____
_____

Quotation Source Information:

_____

_____
_____

April 16
October 16

"We never get a second chance
to make a good first impression."

Unknown

List the names of three people that you trust and who are really close to you:

1. _____
   _____

2. _____
   _____

3. _____
   _____

Ask each of them to describe the first impression that you present.

_____
_____
_____

Write down the top three things that you will change about your first impression:

1. _____
   _____

2. _____
   _____

3. _____

_____

Six Months Review:

_____

_____

_____

April 17
October 17

"The difference between a successful person and others
is not a lack of strength, not a lack of knowledge,
but rather in a lack of will."

Vince Lombardi

What will you do today to improve your ability to be successful?

1. _____
   _____

2. _____
   _____

3. _____
   _____

4. _____
   _____

5. _____
   _____

Six Months Review:
_____
_____
_____

Quotation Source Information:
_____
_____
_____

April 18
October 18

"If everyone is thinking alike then somebody isn't thinking"

George S. Patton

What things do you do to encourage the introduction of new ideas?

1. _____
   _____

2. _____
   _____

3. _____
   _____

What additional things can you do?

1. _____
   _____

2. _____
   _____

3. _____
   _____

Six Months Review:

_____
_____
_____

Quotation Source Information:

_____

_____

_____

April 19
October 19

> "The only limit to our realization of tomorrow
> will be our doubts of today."

Franklin D. Roosevelt

What doubts do you have that is interfering with you overcoming your perceived limits?

1. _____
   _____

2. _____
   _____

3. _____
   _____

What will you do today to begin to eliminate those doubts?
_____
_____
_____

Six Months Review:
_____
_____
_____

Quotation Source Information:
_____
_____
_____

April 20
October 20

"I don't think much of a man who is not
wiser today than he was yesterday."

Abraham Lincoln

What techniques do you use to learn at least one new thing each day?

_____
_____
_____
_____
_____

Six Months Review:

_____
_____
_____

Quotation Source Information:

_____
_____
_____

April 21
October 21

"Here is a simple but powerful rule …
always give people more than they expect to get."

Nelson Boswell

What will you do to ensure that you deliver more than what is expected of you on your next assignment?

_____
_____
_____
_____
_____

Six Months Review:

_____
_____
_____

Quotation Source Information:

_____
_____
_____

April 22
October 22

"Every problem contains the seed of its own solution."

Norman Vincent Peale

Describe your most pressing problem:

_____
_____
_____
_____
_____

Document the first steps of the solution that is visible within the above definition of the problem. Be creative!

_____
_____
_____
_____
_____

Six Months Review:

_____
_____
_____

Quotation Source Information:

_____
_____
_____

April 23
October 23

"We see every problem as a nail if
our only tool is a hammer."

Unknown

What steps are you taking to build up your array of problem-solving tools?

1. _____
   _____

2. _____
   _____

3. _____
   _____

Which new tool will you use today?

_____
_____
_____
_____
_____

Six Months Review:

_____
_____
_____

April 24
October 24

"There is no limit to what you can do if
you don't care who gets the credit."

Unknown

Describe the last situation where you were willing to let someone else
get the credit for an accomplishment:

_____
_____
_____
_____
_____

How did you feel afterwards?

_____
_____
_____
_____

Six Months Review:

_____
_____
_____

April 25
October 25

"Life is a grindstone. Whether it grinds us down
or polishes us up depends on us."

L. Thomas Holdcroft

Describe the three things that life taught you this week:

1. _____
   _____

2. _____
   _____

3. _____
   _____

Six Months Review:
_____
_____
_____

Quotation Source Information:
_____
_____
_____

April 26
October 26

"Courage is doing what you're afraid to do.
There can be no courage unless you're scared."

Eddie Rickenbacker

List three people that you most want to help succeed in their careers:

1. _____
2. _____
3. _____

How will you help them to overcome their fears?

_____
_____
_____
_____
_____

Six Months Review:

_____
_____
_____

Quotation Source Information:

_____
_____
_____

April 27
October 27

"When the student is ready the teacher will appear."

Buddha

Describe a particularly complex problem that you have been trying to solve:

_____
_____
_____
_____
_____

Based on your understanding of the above quote from Buddha, what do you need to do to make the teacher *appear* to educate you on the solution?

_____
_____
_____
_____
_____

Six Months Review:

_____
_____
_____

Quotation Source Information:

_____
_____
_____

April 28
October 28

"The greatest mistake a man can make is
to be afraid of making one."

Elbert Hubbard

List the last three times that the fear of making a mistake held you back:

1. _____
   _____

2. _____
   _____

3. _____
   _____

What do you plan to do to conquer that fear?

_____
_____
_____
_____
_____

Six Months Review:

_____
_____
_____

Quotation Source Information:

_____
_____
_____

April 29
October 29

"The cold reality is that only about 10 to 20 percent of IT projects come in on time and within budget regardless of the process technique that is used."

Wayne L. Anderson

There are a plethora of systems development processes that are available to the systems professional. However, very few systems development projects are successful. What steps will you take to improve the success rate of your project development efforts?

1. _____

2. _____

3. _____

4. _____

5. _____

Six Months Review:

_____
_____
_____

Quotation Source Information:

_____
_____
_____

April 30
October 30

"There is no right way to do something wrong."

Unknown

Name the three most honest people that you know:

1. _____
2. _____
3. _____

What do they do that is different everyone else?

_____
_____
_____

Describe how you can learn from them.

_____
_____
_____

Six Months Review:

_____
_____
_____

May 1
October 31

"He can who thinks he can, and he can't who thinks he can't. This is an inexorable, indisputable law."

Orison Swett Marden

List three things that you wanted to accomplish but didn't think you could:

1. _____

2. _____

3. _____

Now, go get it done!

Six Months Review:
_____
_____
_____

Quotation Source Information:
_____
_____
_____

May 2
November 1

"Time is the scarcest resource of the manager;
if it is not managed, nothing else can be managed."

Peter F. Drucker

Describe the techniques that you use to manage your time effectively:

_____
_____
_____
_____
_____

List three things that you can do to improve on those techniques:

1. _____
   _____

2. _____
   _____

3. _____
   _____

Six Months Review:

_____
_____
_____

Quotation Source Information:

_____
_____
_____

May 3
November 2

> "My best friend is the one who brings out the best in me."

Henry Ford

Name three people who bring out your best qualities:

1. _____
2. _____
3. _____

Which qualities do they bring out the most?

_____
_____
_____
_____
_____

Which quality will you demonstrate to other people today?

_____
_____
_____
_____
_____

Six Months Review:

_____
_____
_____

Quotation Source Information:

_____

_____

_____

May 4
November 3

"Unity to be real must stand the severest strain without breaking."

Mahatma Gandhi

Systems professionals are required to develop a unifying bond between many different people in the organization. Sometimes it is their peers, sometimes their business partners, sometimes their teams and sometimes it is their superiors. Describe a time when that unity was particularity successful:

_____
_____
_____
_____
_____

Six Months Review:

_____
_____
_____

Quotation Source Information:

_____
_____
_____

May 5
November 4

"We have had revolutions and evolutions in warfare, agriculture, industry, and technology and mankind has simply applied, adapted, and adjusted. It is just their way."

R. Wayne Kukowski

What technologies have you implemented that forced your company to adapt to new ways of doing things?

1. _____
   _____

2. _____
   _____

3. _____
   _____

What would you do in the future to allow your company to adapt to the new environment more smoothly?

_____
_____
_____
_____
_____

Six Months Review:

_____
_____
_____

Quotation Source Information:

_____

_____

_____

May 6
November 5

"Build for your team a feeling on oneness, of
dependence on one another and of strength to be
derived by unity."

Vince Lombardi

What will you do to ensure that your team has a feeling of oneness?

1. _____
   _____

2. _____
   _____

3. _____
   _____

4. _____
   _____

5. _____
   _____

Six Months Review:

_____
_____
_____

Quotation Source Information:

_____
_____
_____

May 7
November 6

"One problem thoroughly mastered
is of more value than many poorly mastered."

Booker T. Washington

Describe your problem-solving skills:

_____
_____
_____
_____
_____

Document the one problem that you will begin to thoroughly master today:

_____
_____
_____
_____
_____

Six Months Review:

_____
_____
_____

Quotation Source Information:

_____
_____
_____

May 8
November 7

"Be more concerned with your character than with your reputation. Your character is what you really are while your reputation is merely what others think you are."

John Wooden

List the top three characteristics of your character:

1. _____
   _____

2. _____
   _____

3. _____
   _____

Describe the difference between your character (who you really are) and your current reputation (how other people see you):

_____
_____
_____

Six Months Review:

_____
_____
_____

Quotation Source Information:

_____
_____
_____

May 9
November 8

"A single conversation across the table with a wise man is worth a month's study of books."

Chinese Proverb

List the three wisest people that you know:

1. _____
2. _____
3. _____

Contact each, schedule a meeting and document below what you learned from each.

1. _____
   _____

2. _____
   _____

3. _____
   _____

Six Months Review:
_____
_____
_____

Quotation Source Information:
_____
_____
_____

May 10
November 9

"When you hire people who are smarter than you are, you prove you are smarter than they are."

R. H. Grant

Describe the criteria that you use to hire smart systems professionals:

_____
_____
_____
_____
_____

Describe how you will improve your process for hiring smart systems professionals:

_____
_____
_____
_____
_____

Six Months Review:

_____
_____
_____

Quotation Source Information:

_____
_____
_____

May 11
November 10

"Our aspirations are our possibilities."

Robert Browning

As a systems professional, what are your career aspirations?

_____
_____
_____
_____
_____

What are the next three things you will do, starting today, to make your aspirations possible?

1. _____
   _____

2. _____
   _____

3. _____
   _____

Six Months Review:

_____
_____
_____

Quotation Source Information:

_____
_____
_____

May 12
November 11

"The pessimist sees difficulty in every opportunity.
The optimist sees opportunity in every difficulty."

Winston Churchill

Name three of the most optimistic people that you know:

1. _____
2. _____
3. _____

Describe the behaviors that they display that are different from the other people that you know. Which behaviors will you adopt?

_____
_____
_____
_____
_____

Six Months Review:

_____
_____
_____

Quotation Source Information:

_____
_____
_____

May 13
November 12

"The new information technology—internet and e-mail—have practically eliminated the physical costs of communications."

Peter F. Drucker

What is the most recent systems solution that you implemented that eliminated a cost to your company?

_____
_____
_____
_____
_____

What are two additional system solutions that you can implement immediately that can eliminate costs to your company?

1. _____
   _____

2. _____
   _____

Begin implementing the first solution today!

Six Months Review:

_____
_____
_____

Quotation Source Information:

_____

_____

_____

May 14
November 13

"In this new wave of technology, you can't do it all
yourself, you have to form alliances."

Carlos Slim Helu

How do you go about establishing alliances when you have complex
systems solutions to implement?

_____
_____
_____
_____
_____

Name two people that you feel are very strong at developing alliances:

1. _____
2. _____

Contact each of them today and document at least one thing that you
have learned from each about developing alliances:

_____
_____
_____
_____
_____

Six Months Review:

_____
_____
_____

Quotation Source Information:

_____

_____

_____

May 15
November 14

"The loudest scream I have ever heard was the one in my head as I kept on getting the same error message over and over for no apparent reason."

Peter Biadasz

How easy is it for your business users to navigate around the error messages in your systems?

_____
_____
_____
_____
_____

List the top three things that you can do to improve the interaction between your computer systems and the business user:

1. _____
   _____

2. _____
   _____

3. _____
   _____

Six Months Review:

_____
_____
_____

Quotation Source Information:

_____

_____

_____

May 16
November 15

"You will never know if your constraints are
real or imagined unless you test them."

Wayne L. Anderson

List the top three constraints that are getting in the way of your success:

1. _____
   _____

2. _____
   _____

3. _____
   _____

Describe what you will do to test the reality of those constraints:

_____
_____
_____

Six Months Review:

_____
_____
_____

Quotation Source Information:

_____
_____
_____

May 17
November 16

"It's easy to have faith in yourself and have discipline
when you're a winner, when you're number one.
What you've got to have is faith and discipline
when you're not yet a winner."

Vince Lombardi

Name three people who you admire for having faith and discipline in
the things that they do:

1. _____

2. _____

3. _____

Contact each of them and document at least one activity that they do
that helps them to have strong faith and intense discipline.

_____
_____
_____
_____
_____

Six Months Review:

_____
_____
_____

Quotation Source Information:

_____
_____
_____

May 18
November 17

> "Here is a simple but powerful rule ...
> always give people more than they expect to get."

Nelson Boswell

It is an unfortunate fact that only about 20% to 30% of IT projects come in on time and within budget. What process will you follow to begin to exceed the expectations of your system users?

1. _____
   _____

2. _____
   _____

3. _____
   _____

4. _____
   _____

5. _____
   _____

Six Months Review:
_____
_____
_____

Quotation Source Information:
_____
_____
_____

May 19
November 18

"Learning is an active process. We learn by doing ...
only knowledge that is used sticks in your mind."

Dale Carnegie

It is a requirement of the IT professional to constantly learn new ways
to solve the problems that are presented to them. What steps do you take
to ensure that you are continuously learning and developing as a system
professional?

1. _____
   _____

2. _____
   _____

3. _____
   _____

Six Months Review:

_____
_____
_____

Quotation Source Information:

_____
_____
_____

May 20
November 19

"Make it a *joy* for people to do business with you."

Unknown

List three people with whom you feel it is a joy to do business:

1. _____
2. _____
3. _____

Why is it a joy to do business with them?

_____
_____
_____

What will you begin doing today that will make it a joy for people to do business with *you*?

_____
_____
_____

Six Months Review:

_____
_____
_____

May 21
November 20

"Good is not good where better is expected."

Thomas Fuller

When developing a solution to a business problem, how do you know when *better* is expected?

_____

_____

_____

_____

_____

How do you ensure that you are delivering *better* when it is expected?

_____

_____

_____

_____

Six Months Review:

_____

_____

_____

Quotation Source Information:

_____

_____

_____

May 22
November 21

"If a man knows not what harbor he seeks,
any wind is the right wind."

Seneca

Describe the *harbor* that you are seeking in your IT career:

_____
_____
_____
_____
_____

What steps do you follow to ensure that you are on course?

1. _____
   _____

2. _____
   _____

3. _____
   _____

Six Months Review:

_____
_____
_____

Quotation Source Information:

_____
_____
_____

May 23
November 22

> "You have within you all of the qualities
> necessary for success."

Zig Ziglar

List five of the qualities that are within you that will help you to be a successful system professional?

1. _____
   _____

2. _____
   _____

3. _____
   _____

4. _____
   _____

5. _____
   _____

Six Months Review:

_____
_____
_____

Quotation Source Information:

_____
_____
_____

May 24
November 23

"First impressions are indelibly marked on the fabric of the mind."

John J. Tarrant

What is the first thing that you notice about a person when you meet them?

_____
_____
_____

What is the first thing that another person notices when they first meet _you_?

_____
_____
_____

What do you _want_ them to notice?

_____
_____
_____

Six Months Review:

_____
_____
_____

Quotation Source Information:

_____
_____
_____

May 25
November 24

"Good management consists in showing average people how to do the work of superior people."

John D. Rockefeller

Describe how you go about showing others how to be superior IT professionals:

_____
_____
_____
_____
_____

Describe how you go about developing *yourself* to be a superior IT professional:

_____
_____
_____
_____
_____

Six Months Review:

_____
_____
_____

Quotation Source Information:

_____
_____
_____

May 26
November 25

"Listening well is as powerful a means
of communication and influence as to talk well."

John Marshall

It is imperative that system professionals be extremely good listeners.
You need to be able to listen to the problems and challenges of others
and turn them into workable system solutions. Name three people that
you admire who you feel have superior listening skills:

1. _____
   _____

2. _____
   _____

3. _____
   _____

Contact each of them and document at least one trait that they have that
will help *you* to be a better listener:

_____
_____
_____
_____
_____

Six Months Review:

_____
_____
_____

Quotation Source Information:

_____

_____

_____

May 27
November 26

"Procrastination is one of the most common and deadliest of diseases and its toll on success and happiness is heavy."

Wayne Dyer

List three of the most significant tasks that you are procrastinating on its completion:

1. _____

2. _____

3. _____

Eliminate the first two on your list today!

After the tasks are completed, document how you feel about getting those particular tasks completed.

_____

_____

_____

Remember that feeling the next time you procrastinate on any task!

Six Months Review:

_____

_____

_____

Quotation Source Information:

_____

_____

_____

May 28
November 27

> "I like thinking big. If you're going to be thinking anything, you might as well think big."

Donald Trump

Describe the career levels that you wish to attain as a system professional:

_____
_____
_____
_____
_____

What can you do to make those aspirations bigger?

_____
_____
_____
_____
_____

Six Months Review:

_____
_____
_____

Quotation Source Information:

_____
_____
_____

May 29
November 28

"Imagination is more important than knowledge ..."

Albert Einstein

List three reasons why Albert Einstein's statement is *correct* when it comes to developing system solutions:

1. _____
   _____

2. _____
   _____

3. _____
   _____

Describe how you use your imagination to develop effective systems for your company:

_____
_____
_____

Six Months Review:

_____
_____
_____

Quotation Source Information:

_____
_____
_____

May 30
November 29

"When angry, count ten before you speak;
if very angry, one hundred."

Thomas Jefferson

What do you do in order to avoid displaying anger?

_____
_____
_____
_____
_____

Name three people who you respect for having the ability to control their emotions:

_____
_____
_____

Contact them today and learn their technique.

Six Months Review:

_____
_____
_____

Quotation Source Information:

_____
_____
_____

May 31
November 30

"The way to get started is to quit talking and begin doing."

Walt Disney

Describe a task that you have been talking about doing for a really long time:

_____

_____

_____

_____

_____

List the first three steps to getting that task completed:

1. _____

_____

2. _____

_____

3. _____

_____

Begin executing those steps today!

Six Months Review:

_____

_____

_____

Quotation Source Information:

_____

_____

_____

June 1
December 1

"There is a reason why you hired them."

Wayne L. Anderson

List the specific ways that you manage your people like professionals:

1. _____
   _____

2. _____
   _____

3. _____
   _____

How do you plan to eliminate *micro-management* practices and capitalize on the creativity of your people?

_____
_____
_____
_____
_____

Six Months Review:

_____
_____
_____

Quotation Source Information:

_____
_____
_____

June 2
December 2

"Patience means self-suffering."

Mahatma Gandhi

IT professionals are constantly required to be patient in the pursuit of their endeavors. Describe a time when that patience caused self-suffering:

_____
_____
_____
_____
_____

What did you learn from that experience?

_____
_____
_____
_____
_____

Six Months Review:

_____
_____
_____

Quotation Source Information:

_____
_____
_____

June 3
December 3

"Tact: the ability to describe others as they see themselves."

Abraham Lincoln

List three people who your truly respect their ability to be tactful:

1. _____
2. _____
3. _____

Contact each of them and learn at least one tactful technique from each of them.

1. _____
   _____

2. _____
   _____

3. _____
   _____

Six Months Review:

_____
_____
_____

Quotation Source Information:

_____
_____
_____

June 4
December 4

"Every man of action has a strong dose of egoism, pride, hardness, and cunning. But all those things will be regarded as high qualities if he can make them the means to achieve great ends."

Charles de Gaulle

List three people that you believe are people of action:

1. _____
2. _____
3. _____

Describe what traits that have that are different from other people:
_____
_____
_____

What will you do today to become more of an action oriented IT professional?
_____
_____
_____

Six Months Review:
_____
_____
_____

Quotation Source Information:
_____
_____
_____

June 5
December 5

"Holy cow, I can remember using a manual adding machine and typewriter with carbon paper and I am only sixty-three years old."

Richard Possett

As system professionals, we see many changes in technology on a regular basis. What technologies were prevalent when you started in the information technology field?

1. _____
2. _____
3. _____

Describe the areas where you have most developed as a system professional since you started in this field:

_____
_____
_____

Where do you need further development?

_____
_____
_____

Begin the development process today!

Six Months Review:

_____
_____
_____

Quotation Source Information:

_____

_____

_____

June 6
December 6

> "It's not whether you get knocked down;
> it's whether you get up."

Vince Lombardi

Describe a time when you let a setback get the better of you:

_____
_____
_____
_____
_____

What will you do differently?

_____
_____
_____
_____
_____

Six Months Review:

_____
_____
_____

Quotation Source Information:

_____
_____
_____

June 7
December 7

"This is the nature of genius, to be able to grasp the
knowable even when no one else recognizes
that it is present."

Deepak Chopra

Describe a situation where you saw a solution to a problem that, to you
was obvious, however, others couldn't see it:

_____
_____
_____
_____
_____

How did it make you feel?

_____
_____
_____

Six Months Review:

_____
_____
_____

Quotation Source Information:

_____
_____
_____

June 8
December 8

"Let me assert my firm belief that the only thing
we have to fear is fear itself."

Franklin D. Roosevelt

What things do you fear?

1. _____
   _____

2. _____
   _____

3. _____
   _____

What will you do today to begin to alleviate those fears?

_____
_____
_____
_____
_____

Six Months Review:

_____
_____
_____

Quotation Source Information:

_____
_____
_____

June 9
December 9

"We must build a new world, a far better world—
one in which the eternal dignity of man is respected."

Harry S. Truman

What are you going to do today to improve things for you and your
teammates?

_____
_____
_____
_____
_____

Six Months Review:

_____
_____
_____

Quotation Source Information:

_____
_____
_____

June 10
December 10

"You can't hold a man down without staying down with him."

Booker T. Washington

What will you do to ensure that the people with whom you work can achieve their full potential?

_____

_____

_____

_____

_____

How will you teach others to do the same?

_____

_____

_____

_____

_____

Six Months Review:

_____

_____

_____

Quotation Source Information:

_____

_____

_____

June 11
December 11

"Don't measure yourself by what you have
accomplished, but by what you should have
accomplished with your ability."

John Wooden

Describe the additional things you could have accomplished last week
had you been working at your full potential:

_____
_____
_____
_____
_____

Look at your To Do List for this week. List three additional things that
you will accomplish:

1. _____
   _____

2. _____
   _____

3. _____
   _____

Six Months Review:

_____
_____
_____

Quotation Source Information:

_____

_____

_____

June 12
December 12

> "Regardless of which route that you take,
> the view from the top is the same."

Wayne L. Anderson

Most systems professionals determine early in their career that they want to attain the Chief Information Officer level or higher within their corporation. However, their progress is impeded when they think that they must follow the same path as the person who currently holds that position. This is generally not true and is an imagined barrier.

How will you develop your own path to the level that you want to attain?

_____
_____
_____
_____
_____

Who will you get to help you to develop your path?

1. _____

2. _____

3. _____

Six Months Review:

_____
_____
_____

Quotation Source Information:

_____
_____
_____

June 13
December 13

"Never put a half a person on a job."

Peter F. Drucker

Managers sometimes give important assignments to people who they consider to be their best workers. Unfortunately, that usually means splitting a person's efforts and skills among competing important projects. Describe the ways in which you assign work to other system professionals:

1. _____
   _____

2. _____
   _____

3. _____
   _____

What can you do today to improve on your technique of assigning work?

_____
_____
_____
_____
_____

Six Months Review:

_____
_____
_____

Quotation Source Information:

_____
_____
_____

June 14
December 14

"You've got to love what you do to
really make things happen."

Philip Green

Describe how you feel about being a system professional:

_____
_____
_____
_____
_____

Is it something that you really love doing? (Yes/No) _____

Based on the above quote, describe how your answer impacts how you
make things happen:

_____
_____
_____
_____
_____

Six Months Review:

_____
_____
_____

Quotation Source Information:

_____
_____
_____

June 15
December 15

"With computers and receipts it is always the same —save everything."

Peter Biadasz

The data that your business users store within the systems is vital to the operation of the business. Therefore, the integrity and availability of that data, as well as the protection from disaster, is an essential element of the responsibility of the information technology organization.

List three things that you can do to better protect your company's data:

1. _____
   _____

2. _____
   _____

3. _____
   _____

Six Months Review:

_____
_____
_____

Quotation Source Information:

_____
_____
_____

June 16
December 16

"Punishing honest mistakes stifles creativity.
I want people moving and shaking the earth
and they're going to make mistakes."

Ross Perot

Describe how this quote depicts *your* management style:

_____
_____
_____
_____
_____

Document how you handle people making mistakes and the things that you may have to change to be a better IT professional:

_____
_____
_____

Six Months Review:

_____
_____
_____

Quotation Source Information:

_____
_____
_____

June 17
December 17

"Patience is not passive; on the contrary, it is active;
it is concentrated strength."

Edward G. Bulwer-Lytton

Describe your ability to be patient:

_____
_____
_____
_____
_____

List three things that you can do to demonstrate an improved ability to be patient:

1. _____
   _____

2. _____
   _____

3. _____
   _____

Six Months Review:

_____
_____
_____

Quotation Source Information:

_____
_____
_____

June 18
December 18

"Great works are performed not by strength but by perseverance."

Dr. Samuel Johnson

Occasionally, an IT professional is required to handle a particularly *sticky* problem where the solution is critical to the operation of the business. Describe your ability to persevere when dealing with such a problem:

_____
_____
_____
_____
_____

How can you improve your ability to persevere?

_____
_____
_____

Six Months Review:

_____
_____
_____

Quotation Source Information:

_____
_____
_____

June 19
December 19

"Information technology is all about one thing and that is human productivity. It gives us the ability to work harder and smarter with a smaller unit cost of doing business. Without that utility I render IT useless."

Richard Possett

IT professionals inherently spend a great deal of time implementing productivity improvement systems and processes. List the most recent system or process that you believe improved productivity in your company:

1. _____
   _____

2. _____
   _____

3. _____
   _____

Begin to solicit feedback today on additional changes that you can implement to further improve productivity using those previously implemented system and processes.

_____
_____
_____

Six Months Review:

_____

_____

_____

Quotation Source Information:

_____

_____

_____

June 20
December 20

"Supercomputers will achieve one human brain capacity by 2010, and personal computers will do so by about 2020."

Ray Kurzweil

Assuming the prediction of Ray Kurzweil is correct, what will be the impact of such a development on your company?

_____

_____

_____

_____

_____

What will you do to ease your company in the transition to this technological development?

_____

_____

_____

_____

_____

Six Months Review:

_____

_____

_____

Quotation Source Information:

_____

_____

_____

June 21
December 21

"A problem well stated is a problem half-solved."

Charles Kettering

List the steps you use to define an information system problem:

1. _____
2. _____
3. _____
4. _____
5. _____

What can you do to improve your problem solving techniques?

_____
_____
_____
_____
_____

Six Months Review:

_____
_____
_____

Quotation Source Information:

_____
_____
_____

June 22
December 22

"Being busy does not always mean real work. The object of all work is production or accomplishment and to either of these ends there must be forethought, system, planning, intelligence, and honest purpose, as well as perspiration. Seeming to do is not doing."

Thomas A. Edison

Describe how you ensure that your pursuits are moving your forward and not just busy work:

_____
_____
_____
_____
_____

Six Months Review:

_____
_____
_____

Quotation Source Information:

_____
_____
_____

June 23
December 23

"If we all worked on the assumption that what is
accepted as true is really true, there would be little
hope of advance."

Orville Wright

How do you go about challenging the status quo or what is accepted as
true?

1. _____
   _____

2. _____
   _____

3. _____
   _____

Six Months Review:
_____
_____
_____

Quotation Source Information:
_____
_____
_____

June 24
December 24

"When one door closes another door opens; but we so often look so long and so regretfully upon the closed door, that we do not see the ones which open for us."

Alexander Graham Bell

Describe the most recent situation where it appears that a *door* has been closed to you:

_____
_____
_____
_____
_____

Describe the door that has *opened* as a result of the door that has closed:

_____
_____
_____
_____
_____

Six Months Review:

_____
_____
_____

Quotation Source Information:

_____
_____
_____

June 25
December 25

"I feel sorry for the person who can't get genuinely excited about his work. Not only will he never be satisfied, but he will never achieve anything worthwhile."

Walter Chrysler

Describe what you do to stay excited about your information technology work:

_____
_____
_____
_____
_____

Six Months Review:

_____
_____
_____

Quotation Source Information:

_____
_____
_____

June 26
December 26

"If someday they say of me that in my work
I have contributed something to the welfare and
happiness of my fellow man, I shall be satisfied."

George Westinghouse

How will people describe the information technology work that you
have done?

_____
_____
_____
_____
_____

How will your improve upon what is being said?

_____
_____
_____
_____
_____

Six Months Review:

_____
_____
_____

Quotation Source Information:

_____
_____
_____

June 27
December 27

"You push the button, we do the rest."

George Eastman

What steps do you follow in order to *hide* the complexity of information systems from your business users?

1. _____
   _____

2. _____
   _____

3. _____
   _____

Six Months Review:
_____
_____
_____

Quotation Source Information:
_____
_____
_____

June 28
December 28

"A professional is a person who can do his best at a time when he doesn't particularly feel like it."

Alistair Cooke

What personal steps do you take to motivate yourself during a time when it is not particularly comfortable to do so?

1. _____
   _____

2. _____
   _____

3. _____
   _____

Discuss this topic with a person who you think is extremely good at self-motivation. Learn what they do.

_____
_____
_____

Six Months Review:

_____
_____
_____

Quotation Source Information:

_____
_____
_____

June 29
December 29

> "If you wait until all the lights are *green* before you leave home, you'll never get started on your trip to the top."

Zig Ziglar

List three *green lights* that you are waiting for in order to progress in your IT career:

1. _____
   _____

2. _____
   _____

3. _____
   _____

Don't wait! Begin your *trip* today regardless of the status of the above items.

Six Months Review:
_____
_____
_____

Quotation Source Information:
_____
_____
_____

June 30
December 30

"Obedience of the law is demanded; not asked as a favor."

Theodore Roosevelt

IT professionals have a greater opportunity to perform unethical acts than most due to their ability to access sensitive information. What do you do to ensure that sensitive information is not compromised?

_____
_____
_____
_____
_____

Six Months Review:
_____
_____
_____

Quotation Source Information:
_____
_____
_____

July 1
December 31

"God grant me the serenity to accept the people I cannot change, the courage to change the one I can, and the wisdom to know it's me."

Unknown

A variation of an excerpt from "The Serenity Prayer" by Reinhold Neibuhr

List one thing that you want to change about you:

_____
_____
_____
_____
_____

Do it!!!

Six Months Review:

_____
_____
_____

Quotation Source Information:

_____
_____
_____

Congratulations!!!

You have just completed a magnificent milestone in your life and made a major, but worthwhile, personal investment. By finishing the first six months of the exercises, you have learned a lot about yourself. The knowledge that you have gained will make you a much more powerful IT professional.

If you have concluded the last six months of this book, you have accomplished a long journey that has refined and enhanced your business skills. Furthermore, you have established personal habits needed to further your successful journey in the field of information technology.

Now that you have come to journey's end, share what you have learned with others in your circle of influence, i.e. managers, technicians, friends, and family. By helping others to become more powerful, you make yourself a power person.

There is no doubt IT professionals are givers. By reading and studying the material in this book, you have much to give. Pass forward your knowledge not only to your co-workers, but to everyone that you come into contact in your daily life. Again, congratulations!

Peter Biadasz, Richard Possett and Wayne L. Anderson

Conclusion

You have finished the footwork, so now is the time to put your new knowledge into effect. That is, make it work for you in your IT career. In the first six months, you have fully completed each daily lesson. In the second six months, you have carefully reviewed the assignments and made the appropriate adjustments. Finally, you have absorbed the quotations and learned about the author or the quote source. Over this period of time, you have practiced what you have learned. All of these concluded tasks have made you a more powerful person in the IT world. You did it on your own. Most likely, you did it in private. You were diligent and assiduous. Now, fully infuse this power into your daily life. Release the power of what you've learned into your personal and professional universe.

Indubitably, you already know that powerful IT professionals are power people. You read about them in books, magazines and newspapers. They are all around you in the workplace. They have been your mentors and teachers. So, if you have carefully read this book and studied the materials, then you have made the choice to be powerful. You were exceptional when you purchased this book. You were unique when you finished the last assignment. Now, it is time to truly be a powerful IT professional. Go forth and live the experience. Share your knowledge with your personal acquaintances and professional associates.

Index of Individuals Quoted

Index of Topics Quoted

Note: Many quotes may fit into more than one category.

About the Authors

Peter Biadasz (pronounced *bee-ahd-ish*) has been teaching groups and organizations for nearly two decades. As a teacher, Peter not only shares his vision for each organization he addresses but carefully leads the members to fulfill the vision in a manner that creates win/win scenarios that are in the best interest of the organization. Having taught leadership and networking skills numerous times, Peter has been known to utilize his professional trumpet talent to liven up speaking engagements.

Peter is a graduate of Florida State University. His passion for and expertise in the area of people networking has aided many over the years. Teaching and the skills required to become a great teacher are essential in becoming a master networker. Experience has shown that the people and groups working with Peter have an increase in the quality of many key skills. Furthermore, an excitement for the topics at hand, as never before seen, emerges as those involved transform into distinguished and mature leaders.

The father of an incredible son and precious daughter, Peter is also the author of *MORE LEADS: The Complete Handbook for TIPS Groups, Leads Groups, and Networking Groups* and co-author of the Power Series, of which the book you are reading is a part. Please visit with Peter at www.getmoreleads.net or www.bepowerful.net.

Richard Possett is a forty-five year experienced entrepreneur and seasoned executive from the international financial and insurance services industries. As a successful businessman, Richard has spent decades managing people into new endeavors and to greater heights of performance. Throughout a long and industrious career, one of his guiding expressions has been: "hard work is smart work." As a small business owner and executive, Richard has personally overseen the development and implementation of myriad information systems and controls with the skilled assistance of IT professionals.

Richard was born and raised in Grand Rapids, Michigan. He lived and worked for five years in Los Angeles, California, before moving to mid-America where he and his family have resided for the last eighteen years.

Richard graduated from Western Michigan University with a BBA degree earning a major in accountancy. He is a CPA, small business owner, accredited mortgage loan originator, financialist and past SEC-registered securities representative and licensed insurance agent.

Richard is a former international rugby player. He served in the United States Army during the Vietnam War. He has been married to his best friend and mate for more than forty-one wonderful years. The couple has three awesome adult children, three beautiful young grandchildren and a great son-in-law. Richard's interests are reading, writing and jog-walking with his wife and their two golden retrievers Jordie and Doolie.

Richard is an award-winning author. For a complete catalogue of his literary works, visit www.bepossettive.com. To personally contact the author, please feel free to email him at richard@bepossettive.com. He would love to hear from everyone, everywhere.

Wayne L. Anderson is the President and Chief IT Strategist at Anderson Professional Systems Group, LLC, an IT management consulting company that he founded. APSG specializes in improving the value of the information technology organization.

Wayne has over thirty years in the information technology (IT) industry. He's been a senior IT executive for the past fifteen years. He is a senior executive with an equal blend of technical, business and managerial skills developed during experience with several Fortune 500 companies. He works with senior IT professionals and corporations to further their long and short-range goals using information technology. He provides extensive experience in managing multi-million dollar budgets and large professional IT staffs. Wayne also possesses the unique ability to attract, retain and motivate outstanding management and professional personnel.

He is the author of *Unwrapping the CIO: Demystifying the Chief Information Officer Position*. He is a keynote speaker at a number of professional organizations and academic institutions. In addition, he coaches CIOs on the techniques necessary to be successful in their position.

You may connect with. Wayne Anderson through his professional network on LinkedIn.com using the URL address http://www.linkedin.com/in/ciounwrapped. You may email him at wayne@aspg-ltd.com.

About the Power Series Books

The Power Series Books mean what they say and say what they mean. They are powerful and contain the dynamism to make people like you more powerful. The books are about the reader learning how to effectively acquire and utilize productive power in their life. The books are not concerned with dominion, authority and control. These books are about health, wealth and happiness. The Power Series Books provide the principles that can produce a full and highly successful lifestyle.

There are many elements that make a powerful person such as relationships, leadership, networking, teaching, listening, learning, spirituality, character and health. The aforementioned areas make a short and incomplete list of what it takes to be a powerful person. The syllabus can go on at infinitum. Power Series Book titles include:

Powerful People Have Powerful Character
Powerful People Overcome Powerful Failures
Powerful People Play Powerful Golf
Powerful People Have Powerful Health
Powerful People Are Powerful IT Professionals
Powerful People Are Powerful Learners
Powerful People Are Powerful Listeners
Powerful People Are Powerful Leaders
Powerful People Have Powerful Money
Powerful People Are Powerful Networkers
Powerful People Are Powerful Performers
Powerful People Have Powerful Personalities

Powerful People Have Powerful Relationships
Powerful People Are Powerful Risk Managers
Powerful People Are Powerful Teachers

More Titles To Be Released Next Year

To learn more about the Power Series as well as order additional Power Series books please visit www.bepowerful.net. The Power Series books are the production of Peter Biadasz and Richard Possett. You can learn more about them in the *About The Author* section of the book you are holding.

978-0-595-41753-7
0-595-41753-1